Living
in
Pieces

Isabella Sky Shea

Fulton Books
Meadville, PA

Published by Fulton Books 2023

ISBN 979-8-88982-652-1 (paperback)
ISBN 979-8-88982-653-8 (digital)

Printed in the United States of America

Dedicated to my mother
I love you.

Author's Notes

At the beginning of the pandemic, I began to struggle with my mental health. As the pandemic continued, I started to feel very secluded from the world and developed depression. Throughout my battles with depression, paired with self-harm, I found an outlet in writing poetry. Whenever I was having a hard time comprehending my thoughts or feelings, I would write a poem. There were times when I felt hopeless and wanted to give up. Every time this happened, I would fall back into my writing. The more I wrote, the more I began to understand myself. I have come a long way. I still deal with my depression, but I no longer am ashamed. I'm not defined by my struggles; they are only one step on my path of life. I want others to know that they are not alone. There are so many things to live for; people need you here.

I hope that my poetry collection will benefit others who felt as I did.

Some of the poems in the collection are personal—my thoughts, dreams, fears, and wishes. Others are meant to hold one another together, interlocking the group selected to shine. You will be able to relate to the words you read. The goal is to feel connected to me. Feel how I feel going through the days, one at a time. Consider the path that shaped you. Consider all the thoughts swirling around in my head in your head as well. I would like to believe you will walk away from *Living in Pieces* with a new take on the world, a new view of what goes on around you. You do not need to feel a specific way as you read through my thoughts. Happy, sad, or hurt—all are okay. My writing is yours to read how you wish. Read what you want to.

Consider what you need to. Enjoy all that is in between.

Prologue

One word at a time and you will find your words.
One word at a time and you will find your voice.
Your voice will take you to many places.
Many different people you will find on your journey.
All you have to do is hold what you value and love close.
Follow your heart and love the little things.
Little things hold great power of the
change you can make in this world.
You will make a change.
Be one with the change you want to make.
Don't let the change take away from you.
You are you.
Be you.
Be strong.

Childhood

When you are little, you are untouchable,
You are in a bubble of happiness.
I loved my bubble.
But when I look back now,
I can say with full confidence that my
bubble popped too early.
I don't know if there was anything I
could have done to delay it either.
Could I have held on longer?
I will never know.
How about your bubble?
Is it okay?

Life Limbo

Living a double life.
Everyone has a double life,
Some people have double lives that are similar.
Others don't share anything.
Parallel worlds.
Never overlapping.
What you decide to overlap, it's only up to you.
Most like to have their double lives never cross,
One on this side
One on that side.
What if you couldn't pick?
I couldn't pick,
Others influenced the decision.
Did you get to pick?
Or did someone else get to?

Individualism

Breath.
One breath can save you.
No one has to tell you to breathe at night.
Your body knows
How to breathe without you.
How to live without you.
In a way, your body doesn't need you.
You need your body.
More than your body needs you.
You are, without your body.
Nothing.
One free soul,
In the world.
Would you like that?
Freedom from your body?
Mirrors would no longer stop,
And stare back.
Telling you to change.
You would be free.
Do you want the mirror?
Does the mirror want you?
Do you want to change and leave the mirror behind?

Greater Picture

I was very small.
Four years old.
I went to a preschool that allowed kids to pick the day plan.
If we went outside,
—Painted,
Read stories—
This was all chosen by us.
Some ways one could say this was my first
glimpse into a world of being "independent."
I don't think so.
I believe my "independence" came way before preschool.
When did your
Independence come into the frame?

Colorless

No more dreams.
No more memories of the night.
No more wishes.
No more waking up trying to remember.

No more seeing walking through your head at night.
No more dreams.
No more dreams would be sad.
Do you dream?

All that is left is a soft buzzing of darkness with
No dreams.
All that is left is quiet.
All that is left is sleep.
No dreams, no imagination.

Power

Waterfalls are beautiful.
Each year an estimated 684,000 individuals die
From falls globally.
Are they still beautiful?
Divine?
Elegant?
Exquisite?
What about gorgeous?
Are they still considered artistic?
Yes.
One does not look at a waterfall and see:
Ugly.
Gross.
Hurtful.
Why not?
They have caused pain and loss.
If a person did the same,
Shame and hate would follow.
Is that okay?

Trustless

Beauty is a gift.
Not a "given,"
Or an item handed to one,
Like some believe.
Similar to beauty, trust is a gift.
Trust can be earned,
Just as fast lost.
When you trust someone you are putting yourself
In a vulnerable position.
Vulnerability is scary.
Everything in the open,
Exposed to the world.
Anyone can see,
Anyone can look.
There is no hiding when you are exposed.
How can you take back the vulnerability?
—You can't—
That person, or persons, will still know you,
Your past,
Your struggles.
You can't undo that.
But you can stop more trust from forming.
More experiences from being shared.
That's up to you.

Train Tracks

Train tracks can take a person anywhere.
Walk on a train track,
You have the power to go into the unknown.
When I was little I used to walk on train tracks.
I would walk on the rails.
Balancing on the two-inch metal rails.
Pennies were often found on my walks.
Left by others,
Waiting for the train to flatten them.
They wanted an elongated coin.
Some pennies I found
Were so crushed I couldn't get them off the tracks.
I would try for a bit to remove them.
Resulting in me continuing my walk,
Leaving the penny for the next.
Maybe that left penny you found.
Or maybe,
You were the one to try and elongate the penny,
In the first place.
Casing our paths to cross.

Please Forgive Me

Are you scared of being forgotten?
People not saying your name.
Photos of you no longer on living room walls.
Old clothes once worn thrown away.
Does that scare you?
Does being forgotten scare you?
Or do you long to be forgotten?
Report cards pushed under beds.
Your school desk dismantled.
Rugs adoring your room rolled.
Is that what you want?
Do you want to be forgotten?
Everyone has that thought.
Do you?

Secrets

Everyone has secrets.
What is your secret?
What is it that you keep of yourself?
Maybe you shared,
One other person might know.
Or maybe you have kept it for
Yourself.
Only allow your mind to see.
And wonder in the image.
Your thoughts and feelings.
Did you feel better when you shared?
Was the weight lifted?
Was the wound healed?
Sometimes it is.
Others can't be as lucky as you.
Think about your secret.
You have all the power to share.
Don't let anyone take that away from you.
Believe in you.

Inner Beauty

Eyes are beautiful.
One look into any eye can tell you a story.
I have a story in my eye.
You do too.
Is your story happy?
Sad?
Mine is both, happy and sad mixed together.
Becoming one.
Eyes hold so much sadness.
Fear.
One could say they are meaningless.
No one does.
If I told you your eyes
Are meaningless, what would you say?
Would you laugh?
Walk away?
Look down at your shoes?
Or would you agree?
Would you agree?
Would you look me in the eye and say,
Yes.
My eyes are meaningless.
You wouldn't,
You wouldn't because no one would; you follow the clique.

Pandemic

No more pencil smudge lines on hands.
No more broken classroom chairs.
No more hall bells.
No more classes.
No more running through woods trying to catch the bus.
No more late-night work.
No more school.
No more sports bags barely closing.
No more practices.
No more fast starts.
No more races.
No more sports.
No more late-night hugs.
No more.
If everything was to vanish,
Where would it go?
Where would all of the "no mores" go?
What made them go?
What caused them to run?

Perfect Day

Photos hold snippets of memories.
All the photos you have taken hold a memory,
Pressed between the films.
A moment stuck in time.
Perfect.
As you left it before.
Nothing has changed in the photo
since the day you took it.
Smiles still the same.
Laughs still sing through time.
At one point you loved that photo.
That moment you loved so much you wanted to keep it.
Hold it.
Save it.
You look at photos and long to take the photo again.
To be back in the memory,
You want to be in the moment.
Time left the same.
Not one piece of the puzzle is missing.
Because you have all the pieces in your hand.
In the photo you hold.

Thoughts for Tomorrow

Dreams.
Dreams are merely electrical brain impulses.
Pulling on random thoughts and
imagery from your memories.
Memories of the day,
Memories of your wishes,
Hopes.
Dreaming happens in the REM sleep stage.
Muscles become paralyzed.
For twenty minutes the dream has control.
I don't dream.
I don't get to watch my memories and
thoughts, being twisted around,
Forming new memories and thoughts.
My body doesn't become captivated by dreams.
Instead I lay in bed.
With nothing but the night around me.
Holding me.
I used to dream.
I had dreams every night,
Waking up excited to remember them.
One night was my last dream,
The last I would remember.
I didn't even get to savor the dream.

Think Before You Do

Peanut butter.
How did someone look at a nut and think:
I want to smash it.
I want to crush so many I can spread it.
On toast,
In cookies,
With jam.
Did they think about that little nut?
Did they think about the family?
They didn't.
You would have.
You would have sat down and pondered.
Maybe we need to start pondering more.
About all the little things that get
Pushed away.

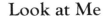

Look at Me

Sitting in class when I was younger.
Not understanding anything.
Getting work handed back.
Red pen.
Everyone else had
Blue pen.
I had red
"Life is hard"
I was told this a lot—still am,
I was told this after "hand back" or tests.
"You will do great things"
Was usually the next commonly used phrase I was told.
The problem no one seemed to have a phrase for was
The great thing.
What was it?
People have phrases for everything.
None for anything I could benefit from.
I know "life is hard."
I don't need a reminder.
"I *will* do great things."
When is the *will* going to change to *have done* great things?
But I did it.
I found my great thing.
All on my own.

Life's Perspective

You're told when you are younger that
Those little things are little things.
That the only "real" problems are big.
People miss that little things can grow,
Or little things can stick together,
Forming one massive thing.
Little things can become harder to fix than big things.
"Big things" all start out as a "little thing."
What about you?
What do you think?

My Photobook

As one can see, life is complex.
That's okay.
It's okay that my life is a jumble of scraps pushed together.
"Okay" is the wrong word.
Not wrong,
Inexact.
My life is unique to me.
No one has the same, or even similar, life as me.
People can share some of my experiences.
They will never know it all.
All the fine details.
Sometimes I try to explain my life to people.
Friends,
Distant relatives,
Teachers,
Colleagues,
They don't understand how to follow.
How to comprehend.
Do you communicate the experiences of your life?

Goodbye

When you lose something important,
You feel the pain in your bones.
Down your spine,
A cold shiver.
People.
You can lose people.
Friends,
Or family.
You don't know you lost something till it's gone.
Too late to go back.
You don't know what you got till it's gone.
What love you had.

Forming Who You Are

Can you fly?
Can you float in the sky?
Sailing through the wind,
The clouds.
Every so often you flap your wings,
To glide.
What color are your wings?
Are they soft as sand?
Strong as glass?
Are you a bird?
Or do you simply hope to fly?
Wish to be the one flying.
Not the one watching.

Soulmate

People can change the way you see that world.
Some people make you see the world
as a happy, safe, equal place.
Others made the world feel scary, uninviting, and grim.
When you meet that one person who makes
the world a better place, you will know
—You will just know—
That person will be that smile on your face
—The song in your head—
The lucky penny on the sidewalk,
A dollar in your back pocket of your favorite jeans,
Faded from years of love.
Finding this person is what can take time.
Have you found that person?

I hope you have.

Life's Gift

I was given a four-leaf clover by a teacher.
She had found them all over the place and gave one to me.
I had never seen a four-leaf clover before.
I had seen them online and knew what they were,
Where they came from,
How they were unique,
Actually holding one in my hand was different.
Twenty minutes after being given the clover,
I was walking home
—A bird pooped on me—
Bird poop is lucky.
With as many birds as there are in the sky,
It's supposedly more rare to be pooped on
by one than it is to win the lottery.
Since that moment, I have kept the clover with me.
Pressed between my phone and my phone case.
I sometimes wonder if this is what happens to
lucky people: clovers being given to them.
Birds picking them out of all the other
pedestrians walking on the sidewalk.

Beach Walks

A perfect day.
One day where everything goes smoothly.
Every moment can be remembered,
A smile to show to go along.
You can look back at the day,
Happy and giddy.
I haven't had a perfect day.
Have you had a perfect day?
Do you think about that day?
Are you proud of the day?
All the good experiences shared?
Who was in your day?
Who was it that got to make the day with you?

Own Path

I'm a butterfly.
Moving and forever changing.
Everyone when they die has a new life they begin.
In my new life I believe I would become a butterfly.
Not just any butterfly, a green one.
Green and yellow—black spotting adoring the left wing.

Why a butterfly?
They are free.
Free from drama and hate,
Flying to places of love.
Green is the color of few lucky butterflies,
One out of sixty-two, I would be that one.
I would be that small piece of luck.
Butterflies' wings are different.
Similar to zebras or fingerprints.
—Unique—
Most butterflies' wings are symmetrical, mine wouldn't.
My wings would be different.
Left and right not matching or fitting
together quite correctly.
Instead they would stand alone.

Respect

Sometimes in life,
The only way to understand someone is to be in their
Thoughts.
To feel what they are feeling,
See what they are seeing,
Experience what they have experienced.
Walk in the shoes of someone else,
Step into their life.
Step into their life and be them,
For one second.
Only one second.
Be them.
Don't lose yourself in them.
Keep them close and yourself closer.

Peace

The peace rose.
How can a flower make peace?
When you give a flower you can ask for forgiveness,
Not peace.
Peace is a concept of social friendship and harmony.
Peace is in the place of
Hostility and violence.
Yet one flower is called
The peace rose.
A large flower of light yellow cream,
Slightly flushed at the petal edges with crimson pink.
Who had the power to give to the rose?

Tears on Cheeks

Sorrow.
The purple hyacinth is a common symbol of sorrow.
Who decided to make a flower live up to that?
To be able to hold all the sorrow.
All the forgiveness and sorrys.
Purple hyacinths are pretty.
Soft purple petals.
Teams of six in each cluster.
Are they pretty enough to hold all the sorrow?
No.
Someone looked at that flower one day:
They thought the flower could.
It can't.
I can't.
You can't.
We can't because nothing can.
Nothing can hold all the sorrow.
Sorrow is too big to be held.

Crayon Box

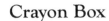

Gladiolus.
Gladiolus, the flower of strength.

Strong stem,
Big flowers.
Light and thin petals.
Over two hundred and fifty shades.
Reds.
Pinks.
Blues.
All the flowers are different.
Different and matching with one another.
All hold strength.
All form one bond.
People are all different.
All hold strength.
Together we form one bond.

Dancing in a Rainbow

Color.
Every day we are surrounded by different colors.
You are a color.
Your hair.
Your skin.
Your eyes.
You wear color on your clothes.
You put color on your face.
You breathe color in the air.
Even black and white are colors.
When you get the option of
Color or black and white.
Either way, you are picking color.
Every single time you are picking color.
We as humans are drawn to colors.
We follow color.
We long for color.
You hold color in your hand and love that color.
What is your color?
What is that color that you could hold forever?
What is the shade
You see yourself in?
As you dance in front of your bedroom mirror.

Mirrored

You have never seen yourself.
You have never seen yourself in person.
All you see is a reflection of you.
Or a photo.
You will never see how others see you.
You can't.
You are you.
They are them.
Different people.
Different views of you.
One person but seen as many,
By multiple people.
You have a view of everyone else.
They don't have that.
They can't see themselves.
You can't see yourself.
Instead you see them for them.
They see you for them.
Who sees you?
Who do you see?

Seeds of a Person

Snowflakes are never identical.
There can never be a twin snowflake.

Start with two identical crystals.
By the time they reach the surface.
They are no longer identical.
Conditions change the snowflake.

Conditions change people.
The way you start as a baby,
The way you are now,
Is different.
No longer identical.
What conditions made you?
Who shaped you,
Into you?

Hourglass

Time.
Seconds and minutes,
Hours and days.
Never to be seen again.
Time is the most precious thing in the world.
The greatest gift you can give to someone,
Your time.
Give the people you love your time.
Pick who you want to spend your time with.
Spend the time you have doing what you love.
With whom you love.
You can never get your time back.
Spend your time wisely.
You don't know how much you have left.
Time is yours to live with.
Whom is your time spent with?

Escaping Reality

I run so I can escape.
Wind in hair.
Rain on tongue.
Striding through woods and grass,
I run.
Sometimes I will run until my legs burn,
Screaming at me to rest.
Crying for my body to pause.
You have an escape.
I run.
Do you run?
Running to stop the thoughts.
Thoughts that play tag in my brain,
I'm never who is chasing.
Only the one running.
I don't like this game,
But I didn't make the rules.
You did.
I run.

Monsters

Monsters hold power,
Over you and I.
You are a monster.
You have power over me that I can't escape,
I try,
But fail.
You are the monster in my mind.
Telling me what to eat,
Drink.
Wear.
Say.
Do.
Be.
I never let you in my mind,
You came unwelcome,
Unannounced.
I take pills to shut you up.
Still you speak.
When will you learn that you are not welcome?
Not invited to the party,
That is my mind.

Forgiveness

How do you tell your mother,
You are leaving?
Not going on a trip,
Vacation.
Voyage.
You are never coming back.
You made me want to leave.
Say goodbye,
Kiss Mom on her cheek.
Hug Dad.
One last time.
You are the reason I wanted to leave.
You took over my mind.
Body.
Soul.
You took all that I had.
Turned it into yours.
I'm taking it back.
You no longer control me.
I can no longer feel you surging through my
Being.

Hello

People are walking away.
Riding bikes.
Cars.
Trucks.
Trains.
They are leaving with no note,
No wish of coming back.
130 people dying each day.
130 people walking away from their life,
Future.
Loved ones.
Dreams.
I was going to be one of those 130 people.
I was able to fight you.
Tune out your words and actions.
You have left scars,
Cuts and bruises.
But I still stand.
I still get to say hello each morning.
130 people dying each day.

Love

Love can change the outcome of anything.
Love changed the outcome,
Love made me want to fight back,
Love caused me to think.
Stop and think.
Understand you are only in my mind.
I do not see you on the streets,
In the stores,
At the park,
I only see you in my mind.
My mind is what makes things scary.
You make things scary.
I am scared of you.
I am scared of what you will do to me if I listen.

Covid

Covid trapped me with my thoughts,
I was left to fend for myself.
Every day I had to prepare to fight.
I fought you every day.
I still fight you every day.
I have learned that I can fight as a
Team.
You are only one thing,
One nuisance.
That nags me.
Day after day,
You nag and nag.

Thank You

In a way, I can say thank you,
Thank you for shaping me.
You made me want to be standing on the ground.
Grass tickling my feet.
I needed you to see,
That I want to be standing on the ground.
We have battled for many moons.
Many suns,
Yet.
Still.
I want to be standing on the ground.

Water

Water is scary.
When you are near water, you are
Scary.
You make me scared.
One wrong step and feet go under.
Shines.
Thighs.
Waist.
Ribs.
Neck.
Chin.
Mouth.
Nose.
All could go underwater.
You want me to go underwater.
I will keep my head up,
I will not let you make me,
Take that step.
The wrong step.

Bold

You are a highlighter.
Bright.
And powerful.
I'm the paper you cover.
My paper is running out.
Soon you will flip my list page,
Before the page turns,
Revealing the blank back.
Your color will slow.
Stopped midline,
Midsentence.
You and I play a game.
Tag is just one.
We race to the end of the pages.
Except I will win.
I will beat you in my game.
I call this game life.

Small Beads of Life

As one grows,
Develops and changes.
They collect beads.
Those beads hold all the memories,
All the experiences of the life they had.
You are just one of the beads.
You are not my first bead.
Nor my last.
You are merely a roadblock.
One bead that paused the rest from being strung.
Now your bead is intermixed.
There is no longer the wall blocking the rest.
Sometimes your bead falls off.
I pick you up.
I will hold you in my hand and remember,
I will remember.
The pain you made.
But I will always restring you.
Because you are one of my beads.
One of the beads that form my life.

Fresh Start

You got a fresh start,
A redo.
What did you do better?
I never got a redo,
You came back stronger.
I had let my guard down,
I got a fresh start because you came back,
Stronger.
More powerful.
When we went to battle, I had to try harder.
I couldn't take a rest.
I had to ask for help.
Somehow you still won.
You made me crumble.
Cry and fall.

Glass Wall

I made a glass wall around me.
Locked doors with a key,
The door only opened for some people.
I'm learning how to keep my door open,
Propped by a stone.
Stones roll away.
The door will shut, lock, and block the entrance.
I will find a new stone to hold my door.

Depression

You have a hand around my neck,
Squeezing until my eyes close. Tightening with strength.
You are everywhere.
Everywhere and nowhere.
I see you with my eyes closed:
Wanting for me.
I can't seem to get away.
Only when I let you take control do
I stop feeling the suffocation
Of your hands.
You have a hand around my neck.
Day in and day out.

Tree Climbing

When you are in a tree you are free,
Untouchable.
Taller than all,
They stand through life unfazed.
Wind, rain, snow, sun they stand tall.
I wish I could stand tall.
As a young child, I climbed trees.
In trees I was untouchable.
I was greater than all below me.
Climb a tree and you will feel the sensation.

Middle Ground

Faces hold emotions.
Emotions are what allow others to understand you.
My face holds few emotions.
I don't cry in front of people.
When tears form in my eyes, they do not fall,
Down my cheeks,
Onto my upper lip.
The tears never form.
Only when I let my guard down do they fall freely.
You are the one who makes my guard stay up.
Your pills have taken all my emotions.
Without the pills, I feel too much;
With the pills, I feel nothing.
Will there ever be a balance?

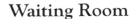

Waiting Room

You sit,
Head in knees.
Shoulders hunched low.
Maybe if you form a small ball with your body,
You will
Disappear.
The hard plastic chair digs into your spine.
Sad faces look at you from across the room.
They hold concern and wonder.
The faces are intrigued by your being.
Little kids point and ask.
Ask their parents why you are sad,
Why is your back pressed firmly against the blue chair?
Your voice is locked in your throat.
You want to answer the questions, but you can't.
You can't open your mouth.
You can't make yourself say a single word.
Instead you only nod or shake your head.
This is how you answer the many questions
that are being asked of you,
By doctors.
Therapists.
Teachers.
Siblings. Friends.
If you open your mouth to speak, the tears will fall.

Slow Motion

You lie in bed with the covers pulled
up and over your head.
The soft blankets hold you.
You are trying to lie still,
Your feet are wrapped around a pillow.
The room is quiet and dark.
You can hear people laughing downstairs.
If you slow your breathing, you can
understand what they are saying.
You see their smiles dance in your mind.
When will you go down?
You won't.
You will stay locked away in your bed.
Voices become hushed; steps make the floorboards creak.
You sense the presence of a heartbeat
outside your bedroom door.
No knock is followed but a line of light across the ceiling.
Your bed bows in with the weight of another body.
The mouth is moving, but you can't hear
What they are saying.
Maybe if you roll closer, you will understand.
But you can't.
Your body is frozen to the sheets.
Eventually, the body gets up and leaves.
You want to call out and ask what they are saying.
But you can't.

Home

The car ride is deafening.
Not with noise but with silence.
Mom has tears in her eyes.
Knees are pressing into your ribs; the
seat belt is crushing your neck.
Outside the window is sun,
Sun that shines on the grass.
Making the horses run through their fields.
Gravel is flying up under the car.
Quickly the car stops, pulled over to the curb.
Mom removes her seat belt and demands that you speak.
You can do nothing to stop the tears
from falling down your face.
You feel defeated but happy.
Happy that you are no longer alone with the monster,
The monster that is your mind.
Mom now holds you as you cry.
She doesn't know why you are crying.
She understands that you don't know either.
She holds you as your guard crumbles to the ground.
You have tried so hard to be strong.
Now you take a deep breath and open your mouth.
You tell of the thoughts that race through your mind.
Mom holds you as you cry.
You are safe in the arms that are your home.
Mom is your home.

Pills

Small, pale, yellow pills.
It's hard to believe that I will take these forever.
One pill every morning with a sip of water.
I could stop.
Then you would come back.
Even with the pills, I find you lurking.
The pills help to drown you out.
Help to dull the suffocative.

Exhaustion

You are tired.
When you wake up in the morning,
your eyes struggle to stay
Open.
You go to bed before the sun sets and still,
You are tired.
You lie in bed watching the night go by.
You are tired.
You can't fall asleep.
You are too tired to do anything.
But when you try to sleep, you can't.
You are tired.

Broken

I am broken.
I am a shard of a person.
All that is left is the glass fragments on the wood floor.
I broke right down the middle,
Split right into two pieces.
Who broke me?
All the people who saw but didn't speak.
All the people who pointed but never asked the question.
All the people who whispered behind
doors but never spoke up.
Everyone, all the people, are to blame.
They are to blame for the glass shards on the wood.
Lots looked.
Many whispered.
Multiple pointed.
But no one asked.
No one spoke up.
With the burning question in their mind.
Now I am broken.
I am split in two.
And they are to blame.
One voice
Held the power.
One chance short.
Now there is glass on the wood floor.

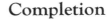

Completion

I did it.
I survived another year.
12 months.
52 weeks.
How do I explain that it was hard
and easy at the same time.
I got good grades.
So it must have been easy.
Right?
It wasn't.
Every single day, I struggled.
It took all my strength to get up each morning.
But you knew that.
Didn't you?
You could tell that in order for me to
complete this year, it took time.
I took longer to do things than I had in the past.
Getting ready no longer took 20 minutes.
Was it because I cared more?
No.
I cared less.

Explanation

You fill your days with tasks.
You are always busy.
I fill my days so I don't have time to think.
If I had free time, I would go crazy.
I need something to do.
I have a mental list in my mind.
Not a list of things to do before I die but
a list that has everything that I
Must do.
I must complete these things.
Graduation is on this list.
I have time limits on my task.
When I need to do things.
When I miss a deadline, I panic.
The one thing that I had control over is suddenly broken.

Just Getting By

Day by day.
Day by day, I take one more step.
These steps led me down the path of life.
I have no idea where my path is going.
Day by day.
If I close my eyes,
I'm walking on a tightrope.
If I spread my arms,
I'm a bird.
Day by day.
Day by day, I take one more step.
My path is narrowing.
You are causing my path to shrink.
You,
You, the monster in my head.
Day by day.
Day by day, I take one more step.
You are right there with me.
I'm running.
Running down my path.
You are winning.
You are always winning.
When will it be my turn?

A Song for You

Your song is of silence.
You sing only for others.
You are holding back what's itching the back of your throat.
You are singing to the clouds outside your window.
Your song is empty.
No words are coming from your mouth.
You are screaming.
Crying and screaming.
Your song is of silence.
You are screaming loudly.
As loud as you can.
No one can hear you.
No one is answering your cries.
Your song is of silence.

Bloodstained Sheets

Dried blood lining your arms.
The blood is brighter than your
Willingness to live.
You stare and feel nothing.
Nothing.
No pain.
No regrets.
Why would you regret the blood?
If there was no blood on your sheets.
There would be no shallow breaths.
People ask you why you make yourself bleed.
If you don't force the blood to flow,
There would be no you in the morning.
No pain.
No regrets.
You sit and watch your blood dry.
You aren't thinking about tomorrow.
You are only thinking about how you are one second older.
Isn't that enough?

Masked

My mask is cracked.
Right down the middle.
The mask that I have worn for so many years is
Broken.
Sadness is no longer hidden.
Smile no longer drawn on my face.
The difference is so obvious.
Has anyone noticed?
No.
Can no one see the gash down my face?
Exposing the hurt and emptiness.
Are they trying to ignore my pain?
Do they not see my scream for help?

Defeated

You have tried.
Tried so hard to make your voice heard.
Each day you become increasingly more exposed.
You reached out to someone,
A handful.
Two handfuls,
Yet still,
You sit alone.
What if you go to a new lunch table?
No.
You have tried.
People still don't see.

Cry for Help

Lava is being poured down my throat,
I scream at the top of my lungs.
I.
Need.
Help.
I stand atop the dining room table.
You are there,
I.
Need.
Help.
Back pressed to the wall.
Arms crossed over chest.
I.
Need.
Help.
You watch me become a fool.
You laugh and smile.
I.
Need.
Help.
You know that I'm going crazy.
I stomp my feet and jump up
And down.
You know I'm losing myself.

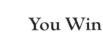

You Win

I give up.
You win.
Feel good?
Feel good that you have destroyed my life.
My family.
I've lost all my friends.
I have nothing and no one.
You did this.
You destroyed my future.
I had things I was going to do.
Memories I was going to make.
You get the gold star.
Take it.

Death Note

A note for me, not you.
You may have won, but I will have the last word.
You may have won, but I'm who they will cry about.
You may have won, but I'm the photo they hang.
This is my note.
I'm sorry.
So fucking sorry.
I tried my best.
I couldn't take the pain.
Anyone who reads this will fall short of understanding.
Only those who fistfight their thoughts will understand.
Only those who wake up crying to be alive will understand.
You make me feel worthless.
How did you do it?
All it took was one thought.
Why am I here?
What is my purpose?
I'm sorry.
So fucking sorry.

Mother's Love

I wish I could take your pain.
That is what my mom told me.
My head was buried in her chest.
I wish I could stop your hurting.
Mom, you can't.
You can't because I don't know how.
I don't know how to give away my burdens.
I never got an instructions manual.
Chapter one.
How to become depressed?
Chapter two.
How do you stop wanting to die?
Chapter three.
Formatting a suicide note.
There is no book that will help.
Mom, you can't take away my emotions.
You can only wipe away my tears.

Forget Me Not

Let's hold hands.
You'll be on my right.
We will both be happy.
On the count of three, let's jump.
Hair flying through the air.
Fingers never unlock.
I feel at peace,
Knowing I will be free soon.
Free from the monster inside.
I toss my head back and laugh.
I'm going to be okay.

The light blinds me.
The spell of my daydream is broken.
Reality is back.
I'm not going to be okay.
The monster laughs.

Change

Green turns brown.
Yellow to gray.
Red to black.
Colors no longer hold beauty.
You have caused the beauty to vanish.
I squeeze my eyes shut,
Hoping that when I open, a rainbow
Will meet me.
The world has been dimmed.
I can't find the switch.
Every turn I take brings me back
To the gray that follows.
Shadows cover the light.

Do You Understand?

Do you know that you hurt others with your pain?
Did you know your grandmother
screamed when she found out?
You didn't.
No one told you.
Let you in on the secret.
That's why people have been hushed.
Why the sudden pause before words.
They are worried.
Worried about you.
Now you know.
You won't change what you are doing.
You are in too deep.
No backing out now.
The scars will still be there.
What's one more now.
One more can't hurt.
You are digging yourself a grave.
But you knew that part.
That's why you aren't scared.

Acknowledgment

During my journey of navigating my mental health, I have had a very extensive support system. My parents, Erin and Tom Shea, had been with me every step of the way. From the first conversation we had about my depression and self-harm, they were ready to bend over backward for me. I appreciate all that you two have done for me, and no day goes by without feeling thankful. Along with my parents, all my friends, siblings, and other family members have been extremely understanding and supportive. I'm so appreciative of all you have done over the years. Thank you. I couldn't have accomplished *Living in Pieces* without you.

Endnotes

Living in Pieces started as one short clipped paragraph. Over the course of several years, many drafts and multiple roadblocks, a finished product broke through the surface. At first, I was hesitant to write something that was so "exposing." These are my thoughts and views on the world. Why would I share them with you? Certainly not type them and turn them into a collection. But that is what I did. I have made my thoughts public.

This poetry collection is signifying the new beginning in my life. A fresh start, if you will. I have come so far throughout my battle with my mental health, and I'm finally ready to put my past behind me and take that next step. I will always struggle with depression and self-harm, but I can confidently say, "I'm okay." I've accepted that my mental health struggles will stay with me. I've also accepted that the only way I can better myself is by moving on.

Over the long course of making my poetry collection, I deleted an abundance of poems. Some I deleted to make the collection flow together; others were too personal. Even though I was willing to write down my thoughts, some thoughts had to be left behind. Your thoughts are your thoughts. My thoughts are mine. You can share your thoughts, and so can I. It is what you pick to hold close that is up to you.

I hope you enjoyed reading through my poems, stepping into my mind.

—Isabella Shea

About the Author

One in three teenagers suffer from a mental health disorder, depression and self-harm being the most common; Isabella Sky Shea was one of those teens. Throughout the COVID-19 pandemic, Isabella faced a personal mental health battle. The separation from other individuals caused Isabella's underlying depression to mutate into whom she calls the monster. The monster caused Isabella to isolate from the rest of her community. After many years of fighting this emotional struggle, Isabella is now a proud survivor of self-harm and depression.

Living in Pieces is Isabella's first publication. Isabella is a young adult who wants other teens suffering to feel less alone. Isabella lives in Vermont with her extensive family and hopes her poems will allow the creation of a safe place for others battling their own mental health monsters. Gaining control of her depression and self-harm may always be a part of Isabella's life. It's Isabella's mission to show others they aren't defined by their physical or psychological scars and to demonstrate a path to resilience.

Many teens suffer in silence. Mental health awareness is increasingly important to help those with no support. If you or someone you know is struggling, call or text 988. 988 Suicide & Crisis Lifeline connects individuals with crisis counselors for emotional support along with other services. Lifeline Chat & Text is available 24-7 across the United States of America and certain territories.

Printed in the USA
CPSIA information can be obtained
at www.ICGtesting.com
LVHW091131310124
770455LV00001B/213